J666

GLASS

Hazel Songhurst

Thomson Learning
New York

Books in this series

Bricks
Electricity
Gas
Glass
Oil

Paper
Plastics
Steel
Water
Wood

Cover: (Main picture) Molten glass slides down tubes into molds at the bottom where air is then blown in to make the glass into bottles. (Top right) Drinking glasses.

First published in the
United States in 1993 by
Thomson Learning
115 Fifth Avenue
New York, NY 10003

First published in 1991 by
Wayland (Publishers) Ltd

Cataloging-in-Publication Data applied for

ISBN: 1-56847-042-8

Printed in Italy

Contents

All the words that appear in
bold are explained in the
glossary on page 30.

What is glass?

Glass is one of the most important materials we have. Glass was discovered a very long time ago, and has been used for centuries to make useful objects. Look around you and see how many things are made of glass. Windows, mirrors, bottles, jars, lenses, and television screens are all made of glass.

Glass is usually a hard, **brittle** material. But when glass is heated it changes. The glass melts and then flows like a sticky liquid.

A long ribbon of hot, liquid glass flows onto a conveyor belt in a glass factory.

Molten glass can be pulled, stretched, and pressed in any direction and made into different shapes.

Glass is a strong, hard material that is made into objects of all shapes and sizes.

When glass is cool, it becomes strong and hard. The glass may feel solid, but it is still really a liquid. Scientists call glass a "supercooled liquid." Like a clear liquid, glass is **transparent**, and light passes through it. All these unusual qualities make glass a very useful material.

How glass is made

Clear glass is made mostly from **silica sand**. This is a very pure, clean type of sand. The other ingredients are **soda ash** and **limestone**. To make glass, they are all mixed together and melted in a **furnace** at a temperature of about 2,700°F.

To make glass, silica sand, soda ash, and limestone are melted together in a furnace.

Glass can be made by using silica sand alone, but much higher heat is needed to melt it.

Left Silica sand piled up outside a glass factory. This is the main ingredient for glass.

Below Heavy lead-crystal glass is made by adding the metal lead to the glass mixture.

Soda ash is used to make the mixture melt at a lower temperature. Adding limestone keeps the finished glass from breaking up in water. Waste glass is also added. This makes the glass mixture melt more quickly.

Different types of glass can be made by adding other materials to the mixture. Adding **lead** makes heavy lead-crystal that is used to make wine glasses. Adding **borax** makes glass that can be heated safely and used for making test tubes or Pyrex containers for cooking.

Blowing glass

The glassblower heats the glass in a small furnace to keep it soft while it is being shaped.

In the past, all glass was blown and shaped by hand. It is a skill that is still used today, and glassblowers blow glass to make beautiful and unusual objects.

To blow glass, the glassblower blows down a long, hollow metal rod, which has a lump of molten glass on the end. The molten glass forms a bubble and is shaped against a stone slab.

The glassblower blows down the hollow rod to make the lump of glass on the end into a bubble.

The glassblower uses tools to cut and shape the handle of this glass vase.

The glassblower cuts off the top of the bubble with shears, and finishes shaping the work with tools. He or she must work quickly to shape the glass while it is still hot. Finally the glassblower removes the metal rod and leaves the glass to cool and harden.

Today, ordinary glass jars and bottles are still made by blowing glass, but it is usually done in a factory by machines that use **compressed air**.

Glass for bottles

Glass is often used to package food and beverages, since it is strong, easy to clean, and does not leak. Computers are used to design the shape for a bottle or jar and figure out how much glass to use.

Bottles and jars are made by blowing glass. The glass is blown **automatically**. To make a bottle, a lump of molten glass called a **gob** is dropped into a mold.

This diagram shows how molten glass is put into molds and blown to make a bottle.

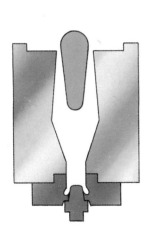 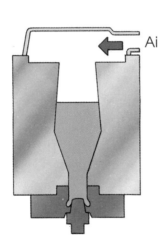 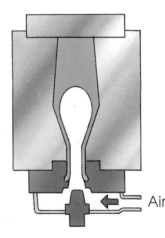 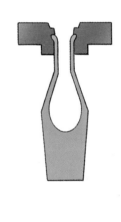

Air

Air

Molten glass drops into mold

Air is blown in from the top to make the neck

Air is blown in at the bottom to make the rough shape

Bottle shape is formed

Air is then blown in, forcing it into a rough shape called a **parison**.

The parison is then put into a second mold, and more air is blown in to make the final shape. The glass bottle is then reheated and cooled very slowly inside a long tunnel called a **lehr**. This is called **annealing**.

The new bottles are carefully checked. Then they are sent to a bottling **plant** where they are filled and sealed and given a label.

Above Finished bottles are carefully checked for any faults.

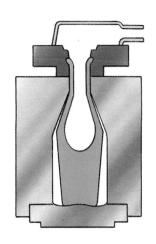
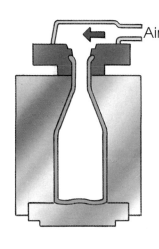
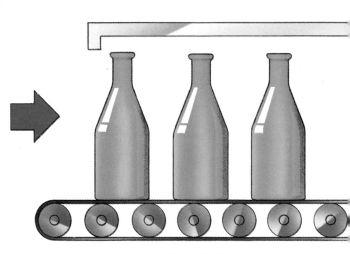

Bottle shape is placed in the second mold

Air is blown in the top to make the finished shape

Annealing lehr for heating and cooling bottles

Making flat glass

The most common use for glass is for windows, since it is strong, clear and weatherproof. But for hundreds of years, making big pieces of flat glass was difficult and costly.

Today flat glass is cheap and easy to make using the **float glass** method. Hot molten glass is floated on top of molten tin in a large tank. The smooth surface of the tin keeps the molten glass layer smooth and flat. The glass is made thicker or thinner by changing the speed at which it flows through the tank.

This diagram shows the different stages for making flat glass.

Glass ingredients

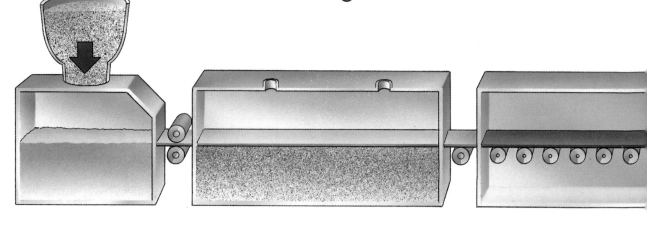

Melting furnace

Glass floating on molten tin

Annealing lehr (heating and cooling in oven)

The flat glass is then heated and cooled very slowly. This is the annealing process and takes place in the long tunnel called the lehr. The flat glass is moved along on rollers to where it is automatically washed, cut into big sheets, and stacked.

Left *A long ribbon of cooled flat glass comes out of the lehr to be washed and cut.*

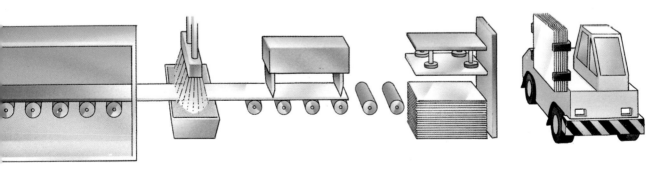

Washing   Cutting   Stacking   Transporting to warehouse

Glass in buildings

In the past, most buildings had windows with small panes of thick, bumpy glass that did not let in much light. Today new buildings are built with big windows to let in plenty of light. This makes rooms look large and cheerful.

Many windows in buildings today are **double-glazed**. This gives good protection against the weather. The walls of some high-rise buildings are made of solar-control glass panels. They are made by altering the ingredients of ordinary glass or covering glass panels with a layer of metal or color coating. This lets the light in but absorbs or reflects the heat. This keeps the rooms inside cool on even the hottest days.

Store display windows are made with big sheets of glass. It is best to use special safety glass in places where there are lots of people because ordinary glass breaks so easily.

It is best to use strengthened glass for store windows on busy streets.

14

This skyscraper in Canada has solar-control glass panel walls.

Decorative glass

Squeezing glass between rollers. The top roller has a pattern cut into it.

Glass is made with different patterns and colors. See how many different kinds of decorative glass you can find at home in doors, windows, bowls and vases.

A decoration for fine glass can be made by cutting the glass on the edge of a fast-moving copper wheel. A sharp point can also be used to scratch the glass surface to make a pattern. Lead glass is often used because it is soft to cut and sparkles in the light.

This craftsman is cutting a pattern on a glass bowl using a sharp copper wheel.

16

A pattern can be made on hot glass by pressing it between metal rollers. This makes the glass into a flat sheet. The top roller has a pattern cut into it, which is rolled onto the glass.

Stained glass windows are made of shapes of colored glass that are fixed together with lead strips.

Colored glass has been used for centuries to make beautiful decorations. The glass is colored by adding metals such as copper or iron to the glass mixture before it is heated. Stained glass windows are made up of small panes of colored glass. These are **soldered** into lead frames to make very beautiful pictures.

Making glass stronger

Above Wire safety glass.

When ordinary glass breaks it smashes into sharp, jagged pieces. This can be dangerous, so special types of safety glass are made.

The first safety glass to be made was wire glass. This glass has a wire **mesh** sandwiched between two sheets of glass. If a building with wire glass in the windows catches fire, the melted glass does not fall but stays stuck to the wire mesh.

A smashed windshield that does not fall into sharp pieces.

To make laminated glass, a clear plastic sheet is sandwiched between two layers of flat glass.

Toughened glass is made using a very high heat so that it is stronger than ordinary glass. Car windshields are often made from toughened glass. If the windshield breaks, it falls apart in small lumps with no sharp edges.

The strongest glass is called laminated glass. A clear plastic layer, or laminate, is laid between two layers of glass. If the glass breaks, the pieces of glass stay fixed to the plastic. Aircraft windshields, which have to be very strong, are often made of laminated glass.

Looking at lenses

Lenses are pieces of curved glass. When you look through a lens, the curved shape of the glass changes the way you see things. This is very useful as it can make things look bigger or smaller.

Some lenses have thick glass in the middle. This makes an object look bigger than it actually is. These are called convex lenses. Other lenses are thin in the middle and make things look smaller. These are concave lenses.

If you look at an object through a convex lens it makes what you see appear bigger.

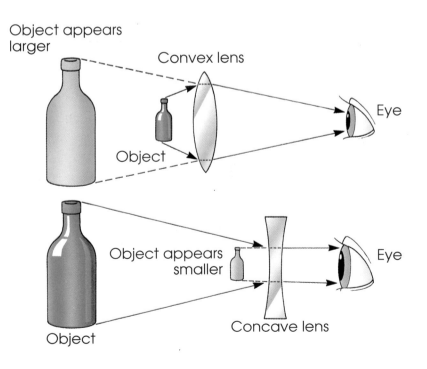

Object appears larger

Convex lens

Eye

Object

If you look at an object through a concave lens it makes what you see appear smaller.

Object appears smaller

Eye

Object

Concave lens

20

The magnifying glass makes the plant look bigger so it can be seen more clearly.

Lenses are made of **optical glass**. Hot molten glass is pressed into shapes called **blanks**. These are carefully ground and polished to the exact size and thickness that is needed.

Lenses are used in cameras, binoculars, telescopes, and microscopes. People with bad eyesight wear glasses. The lens is made to the right shape and thickness to help them see better.

Mirrors

A mirror gives us a **reflection** of what it "sees." Glass is used for making mirrors. The glass has a thin layer of silver on one side. The shiny metal reflects light.

The glass that is used to make a mirror has to be very flat. This is because small curves in the glass alter the reflection you see. Perhaps you have looked in mirrors at fairgrounds where wavy glass is used to make crazy reflections.

Wavy glass mirrors at a fairground pull and stretch this girl's reflection out of shape.

22

To make a mirror, first the sheet of glass is carefully washed. It is then covered with layers of tin and silver and a copper coating for protection. When the layers have dried, the coated side of the glass is covered with two layers of special paint for more protection.

Mirrors have lots of uses. They are often used to make rooms look bigger, or they are tinted and used on the outside of buildings as solar-control glass. Some telescopes use big mirrors to reflect light from the stars. A **solar furnace** uses mirrors to trap and reflect the sun's heat.

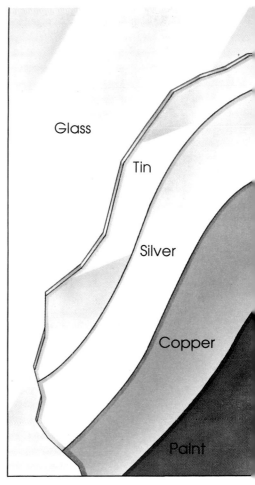

Above *This diagram shows the layers that cover a glass sheet to make a mirror.*

Left *A huge mirror traps the sun's rays to make energy to work a furnace.*

Glass that bends

Glass is a hard, rigid material. But if molten glass is forced through tiny holes it can be pulled into fine, soft threads of glass that bend easily.

These threads of glass are called fiberglass. They can be made into thick matting and used for **insulation**. You may have fiberglass in the walls and roof of your home. Fiberglass is useful because it keeps buildings warm in winter and cool in summer.

These men have put fiberglass into the walls of a new house to insulate it.

Fiberglass can be mixed with other materials to make the material stronger. If fiberglass is mixed with plastic it makes "glass reinforced plastic" often called GRP. This is used to make car bodies and boat hulls because it is lightweight, strong, and waterproof. If fiberglass is mixed with cement it makes "glass reinforced concrete," or GRC. This is a strong material that is often used for building.

Glass reinforced plastic is light and strong. The bodies of Lotus cars are made of this material.

Recycling glass

Glass lasts a long time. Glass bottles can be used again and again. But very often glass is used only once and thrown away. This is a waste of a useful material. It also harms the environment because glass does not break down but remains in the earth forever.

Many people are very concerned about this. In some countries nearly half of the bottles that are used are **recycled**. They are taken to special collection

This diagram shows what happens to glass at a recycling center.

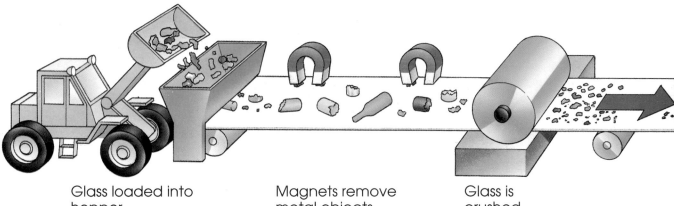

Glass loaded into hopper

Magnets remove metal objects

Glass is crushed

centers. At a collection center, people put their brown, clear, and green glass in different containers. A truck picks up the glass and takes it to a recycling center. Here the glass is washed and crushed.

At a glass factory the crushed glass is added to the glass mixture in the furnace. The glass is melted. Remelting glass uses up much less energy than melting new materials. At the same time, smaller amounts of new materials are needed to make glass. In this way the world's resources are being saved by recycling glass.

Above *Collection centers help people to recycle glass.*

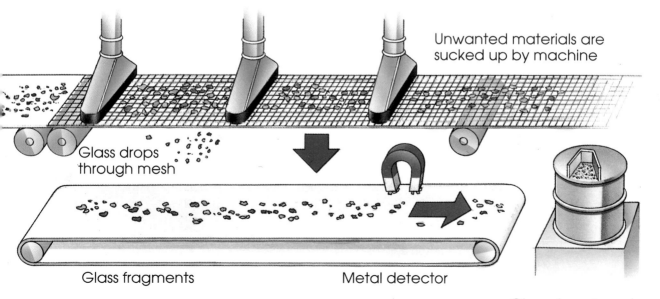

Unwanted materials are sucked up by machine

Glass drops through mesh

Glass fragments

Metal detector

Glass stored ready to go to glass factory

Projects with glass

Musical glass

You will need:

Empty glass bottles of different shapes   A spoon
Water   Drinking glasses

1. Fill some empty bottles with water. Lightly tap the bottles with a spoon to make notes. Vary the amounts of water to make low and high notes.

2. Collect different shaped bottles— some with short thick necks, others with long necks. Try blowing across the tops of them to make sounds. Notice which bottles work best.

3. Wet your finger and rub it around the rim of different-size drinking glasses. Some should produce a note. Experiment to see which is more musical—thick or thin glass.

Make a "stained glass window"

You will need:

Colored acetate
Black sticky tape
Pencil, paper, and scissors

1. Draw a picture or pattern on paper. Keep this design very simple. It is best to draw big, angular shapes. Cut out your paper design and keep all the pieces in position.

2. Use these paper shapes as a pattern to cut out acetate shapes in different colors.

3. Arrange the cut-out shapes on a flat surface in position. Make sure they fit well together. Join the pieces with black sticky tape.

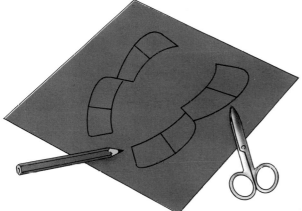

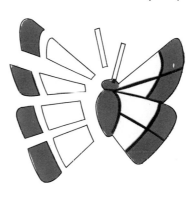

4. Position your "stained glass" on a sunny window and stick down with tape.

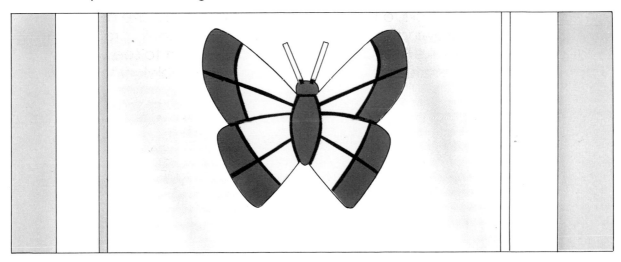

If you hold up a sheet of white paper in front of your "stained glass" you will see colored spots of light reflected onto the paper. On a dull day, shine a flashlight through your design to show this effect.

Glossary

Annealing   The heating and slow cooling of glass in order to make it stronger.

Automatic   Able to move and work by itself. Some machines are automatic, for example.

Blank   A partially shaped piece of glass made by pressing or blowing.

Borax   A mineral that is added to make a very tough glass.

Brittle   Easily broken; fragile.

Compressed air   Air that is squeezed so that it is at a very high pressure.

Double-glazed   Fitted with two layers of glass. Windows are often double-glazed.

Float glass   Flat clear glass made by allowing molten glass to float on tin.

Furnace   An enclosed place that produces very high heat.

Gob   A lump of something soft, such as melted glass.

Insulation   A material that stops the movement of cold or warm air through the walls or roof of a building.

Lead   A heavy metal.

Lehr   An oven in which newly made glass is slowly heated and cooled.

Limestone   A chalky rock that is used in glassmaking.

Mesh   A network of wire.

Molten glass   Hot, melted liquid glass.

Optical glass   A pure, very high-quality clear glass used to make lenses.

Parison   The word for the first shape of a bottle or jar.

Plant   A factory or works where industry takes place.

Recycle   To use again and again; to get or make something useful out of discarded things.

Reflection   Light thrown back from a surface; an image thrown back from a shiny surface, such as a mirror.

Silica sand   The main ingredient of glass. It is found naturally in sand as a material called quartz.

Soda ash   A material that is made in a chemical factory and used in glassmaking.

Solar furnace   A furnace that uses mirrors to trap the sun's rays as a source of heat.

Solder   To use a mixture of heated metals to join metal objects or pieces together.

Transparent   So clear that light can pass through; easily seen through.

Books to read

Cackett, Sue. *Glass*. Resources Today. New York: Gloucester, 1988.

Condon, Judith. *Recycling Glass*. Waste Control. New York: Franklin Watts, 1991.

Kolb, Kenneth and Doris Kolb. *Glass: Its Many Facets*. Hillside, NJ: Enslow, 1988.

Mitgutsch, Ali. *From Sand to Glass*. Minneapolis: Carolrhoda Books, 1981.

Patterson, Alan J. *How Glass Is Made*. New York: Facts on File, 1986.

Useful addresses

National China and Glass
  Giftware Association
1115 Clifton Avenue
Clifton, NJ

National Glass Association
8200 Greensboro Drive, Suite 302
McClean, VA 22102

Index

Picture acknowledgments

The publishers would like to thank the following for allowing their photographs to be reproduced in this book: British Glass 7 (bottom), 16 (bottom); Bruce Coleman Ltd (Fco Márquez) 8 (top), (Jen and Des Bartlett) 18; Greg Evans Photo Library 15, 23; Eye Ubiquitous (John Hulme) 22; Chris Fairclough Colour Library *title page*, 21, 24; Pilkington plc 6, 13, 16 (top), 19; Schott Glass Ltd 4, 7 (top), 8 (bottom), 9, 11, 17; Topham Picture Library *cover* (top), 5; Stephen White-Thomson 27; Zefa *cover* (bottom), 14, 25. All artwork by Peter Bull Art except for page 18 by the Hayward Art Group and pages 28–9 by Janos Marffi.